STOP THROWING STONES:

THE ANATOMY OF A CHRISTIAN PROPHET'S SEX ADDICTION

MATTHEW ROBERT PAYNE

Paperback ISBN: 978-1-64830-295-4

DEDICATION

This book is dedicated to all the sex addicts in the world and the family and friends that pray to see them free. I hope my story sheds some light to bring hope and encouragement.

WARNING

This book exposes the life of a thirty-year sex addiction. Portions of this are not suitable for young audiences. If you are under the age of eighteen, please read no further. It contains graphic sexual content including language, scenarios, and outcomes. Consider this to be an adult only book. The author wrote this book to expose the lifestyle and resulting negative consequences of sex addiction, specifically to prostitutes and pornography. Additionally, certain adults may also find the content offensive. As a result, read at your own risk.

CONTENTS

SPECIAL NOTE ABOUT EDITING

In the past I used a very expensive editor for publishing my books. My ministry income has now halved, and I cannot afford the expense for that quality of editor, so I apologize that the quality of my writing has decreased. I hope that you can appreciate my predicament and that you will still choose to read my books. If you "feel led" to sponsor the editing for a future book with a higher quality of editing, I would appreciate that. Please email me at survivors.sanctuary@gmail.com.

INTRODUCTION

A large proportion of men sitting in churches next to you and standing worshipping beside you have a secret sin called an addiction to pornography. This can also lead to an addiction to prostitutes. These men can be very intimate with the Lord, be very gifted, and may even be a prophet like myself.

This is going to be my hardest book ever.

I want to tell you that it is quite expensive to produce a book. At the moment, I have the money to be able to publish this one. This book in particular was hard for me because I have a reputation in Christian circles. It takes a lot of humility to go ahead and expose my sins and vulnerabilities, especially when I do not have answers to my issues yet. However, if this book helps just one person, then it is worth it. If you're a person who has a sex addiction, who is addicted to prostitutes, or addicted to pornography, then this book is for you.

If you are caught in these addictions and do not have answers, keep reading. The Holy Spirit is compelling me to come forward and say this, that as of March 11th, 2021, I, Matthew Robert Payne, am still a sex addict. But I'm not just writing this book for you though. The Holy Spirit asked me to do this because part of the process of repentance is to confess our sins to one another. So, this is my public confession of the sins that weigh me down the most.

I hope that this very open confession will help many people who read this book. I said right at the beginning that I haven't got answers to these addictions. I'm not currently healed, and I'm not currently free. I therefore wish to put a disclaimer on this book that this is not a book about answers, and this is not a book about how to free oneself from these addictions.

The theme for this book is based James 5:16:

> "Build your faith by surrounding yourself with Christians you trust and who love and encourage you. Regularly confess your sins to one another. Pray for each other. Healing and forgiveness will naturally flow. Anyone *who lives the way God wants* and who learns to *pray effectively, consistently, and persistently,* as a matter of lifestyle, will produce *massive, maximum results.*"

My main point of this book is that there is rampant sexual sin in the church. But this sin is never dealt with because it is kept hidden, and secrecy is its power. But at the times this sin is exposed, the church just throws the stones of condemnation, and without first offering the healing that brings freedom. So, this book is not about answers. Even if I had the answer, how could you apply it? Where in the church are you going to "surround yourself with Christians you trust who love and encourage you?" How are you going to be able to regularly confess these sins to others? Who is going to pray for you since you can't even talk about it? James 5:16 says healing will naturally flow in a safe environment of open, honest confession. Without this environment, instead of healing, sin grows unchecked. And wait until you read the statistics on just how rampant this sin is in the church. Oh. Just wait.

CHAPTER 1: MEETING JESUS

When I was eight years old, we had a family cat named Tinkerbell. I had a father who was a strict disciplinarian and was quite violent. Due to his work schedule, I did not see him often; we were not close. Also, my older brother used to pick on me and was also violent toward me. I was a sad and lonely little boy. Tinkerbell used to come in my bedroom a lot which comforted me. I remember being in my room and crying and talking to her—she understood me. Then Tinkerbell got hit by a car and died. I was devastated. For six months my parents did not replace her because they wanted me to finish grieving.

During this time a children's evangelist came to our church. If you're not a Christian, an evangelist is someone who presents the Christian message about Jesus as the savior of the world and invites people to become a Christian. This was the first time I had ever met an evangelist. He came to our church after school, and I went there to see him. This Christian evangelist talked about how you can have a "special friend" called Jesus. He said He will be your special friend, will never leave you, will always be with you, and you can talk to Him and be really close to Him. Since I'd lost Tinkerbell I was in the market for a special friend. It was particularly comforting that he said this special friend will never leave you, as my cat had just died.

He asked the boys and girls to come forward if any of them wanted to accept Jesus. The evangelist just said, "Come forward if you want to receive Jesus as your special friend." I came forward and invited Jesus into my heart. I was an innocent boy.

For some reason, I quickly developed an ability to hear Jesus. We had song books back in those days called *Scripture in Song*, which included Psalms, Proverbs and different scriptures in the Bible. If you actually looked up the choruses in the Bible, you would find they were word for word. These songs were basically scripture verses put to music. Jesus used to talk to me when I was down or upset. He would answer my thoughts using words from these songs.

Another way He talked to me was through scripture verses themselves. My mother was a Christian and each week she would use a different verse for me and my brothers and sister to memorize. I am the second youngest of four children. I have a younger brother, an older brother and an older sister. My mother would hang a scripture verse on the bathroom mirror for us kids. Every time we brushed our teeth in the morning, we'd read the verse. Then at the end of the week we used to have to quote the verse and the scripture reference. If we didn't do that, we didn't get our pocket money, we didn't get our allowance for the week. Over several years this built a solid foundation for my faith, which included many verses. Jesus would talk to me by bringing up a verse to my mind to help me in a situation, especially when I was feeling down or upset.

So, Jesus had two ways at that time of communicating with me. He used to use the words to the *Scripture and Songs*, and He'd bring up a scripture verse I had memorized. Through these I developed a deep and personal relationship with Jesus.

CHAPTER 2: THE BEACH

I grew up as a surfer in a coastal suburb called Coffs Harbor in the state of New South Wales in Australia. My brother Rodney and I used to go surfing together. Surfing is a very competitive sport, and I wasn't the best surfer by any means. As a surfer I didn't like to compete with other surfers to catch waves. So, I found a less popular beach with smaller waves—this meant less competition.

On one occasion at this beach, I caught a wave that brought me to another smaller beach, separated from the main beach by some rocks close to the water's edge. As I continued riding the wave, I noticed nude women and men walking on this more secluded beach. I was fourteen at the time and had never seen a naked woman before. Needless to say, this got my attention.

I walked up to some of them who were sitting on the beach naked. I started a conversation with them, and they were quite friendly. One of the women said that her niece would be coming to the beach the next week and that I should come down. Her niece was sixteen. When she found out I was fourteen, she said that her niece was a nudist too and that if I came to the beach next week, I would see her niece there. As a fourteen-year-old boy you can imagine how attractive that was to me. I would be able to meet a young girl, and naked at that.

I came down to the beach the next week and I was excited. But it was overcast that day and that particular group wasn't there. Since I was on a nudist beach, I took off my clothes and sat next to a guy. As we began talking, he asked me, "Do you want to go for a swim?" So, I went. It was a different experience going for a swim with no clothes on. When I was swimming naked, he reached down and touched me in my private parts, and it scared me. I ran out of there, put on my clothes, and went home.

I was disappointed with Jesus because I thought I was going to meet a friend, like a little girlfriend on the beach. As I was riding home, I said to Jesus, "If you don't get me a girlfriend on the way home, a girl that can be my friend, I'm going to go back to the beach and be with that guy." I was naïve. I had no idea that decision would lead to life-long downward spiral leaving a trail of devastation.

Jesus doesn't take threats. I want to warn you not to threaten Jesus because it can have catastrophic consequences, which it did for me. I got all the way home, and He hadn't got me a girlfriend, and so I went back to the beach. The guy was surprised that I came back and gave me oral sex. That was the first time I'd had an erection, and the first time I'd ejaculated. Since most people reading this will be guys, I'm going to be forthcoming in this book.

Please excuse me if you're a woman and this is difficult for you, but the idea of oral sex for a guy is pleasurable. Even though it was with a guy, and it was a homosexual act, it was a pleasurable experience for me and something that I wanted to repeat. I imagine that the guy on the beach was in his thirties. Since I was only fourteen, you could call that sexual abuse, and you could call him a predator, but I wouldn't necessarily call him a pedophile. A pedophile could be defined as someone having sexual relations with someone under the age of eighteen. So, you could say he's a pedophile, but I think that he was more of a homosexual that just came across a young guy that was attractive to him. I started to make a habit of going to that beach and having these encounters.

CHAPTER 3: MY FIRST PORN ENCOUNTER

I went to the beach the next weekend since the naked women turned me on. I used to see men there, but we'll talk about that in the next chapter. I knew there were pornographic books and magazines in stores and newspaper shops. So, I bought my first porn magazine. I understood that I could get an erection and I understood, well I worked out, how to masturbate by fantasizing with the pictures. So, I had my first experience as a young, basically virgin, guy masturbating to pornography, and I really enjoyed it.

I can't explain to you what secret desire, need, or emotional wound this fulfilled. I masturbated to the pictures and started buying more pornography. It was like having a substitute girlfriend. I don't know what part of a guy is comforted by looking at pornography and masturbating, but there are a lot of guys that do it. I'll go over the actual statistic later. But it's a lot.

CHAPTER 4: MEETING MEN

I had an excuse for going to this nudist beach as I was ostensibly going surfing. I used to go surfing with my brother at other beaches, but I used to go by myself down to the nudist beach. My older brother never wanted to go to that beach because it wasn't the best beach in town for surfing. I'd go down to that nudist beach and talk to the older women. But I also knew a way of approaching the homosexuals there and have them perform oral sex on me.

Many men would find this repulsive, but a lot of men reading this know about oral sex, especially those addicted to prostitutes. You may think having men giving you oral sex is sick, but I found it pleasurable. I didn't find many other things with homosexuals pleasurable.

On one occasion, a gay man wanted to have anal sex with me, and began to initiate it, but I stopped it. I'm very fortunate that the men I was with at that time didn't force themselves upon me and rape me because that could have happened. I had never had anal sex before. I was listening to a video about a porn star talking about the industry and she said it took about twenty times for her to have anal sex before it stopped hurting her. Apparently, it can stop hurting and become really pleasurable, but I don't think I'd go through those twenty times because it was starting to really hurt when this guy. I never did meet the niece.

I had a relationship with Jesus, but now when I went to church, I stopped singing, and I stopped worshipping. I couldn't worship Jesus anymore and I couldn't sing love songs to Jesus anymore, I just couldn't do it. Some people can be in sin and feel guilty, condemned and shameful and still sing to Jesus and still worship—not me. My whole relationship with Jesus was affected by this. What I was doing brought me so much shame and condemnation. It was seriously affecting my Christian life.

Interestingly enough, at the age of fourteen, as I watched Billy Graham, a famous evangelist, on TV, I felt like Jesus tell me something. As I was watching, I felt as though Jesus told me that I was going to be an evangelist too one day. That was forty years ago. I'm fifty-four and I'm still waiting.

CHAPTER 5: MY FIRST PROSTITUTE

At seventeen, I graduated from high school in a small country town. When I turned eighteen, I moved to the big city, Sydney, Australia. My cousin lived there and worked in the city. I used to walk with him to his work. We got off at the King's Cross train station, which is an infamous red-light district, with many prostitutes.

As I was walking with him to his work one day, a young girl propositioned me saying, "Are you looking for a girl?" I stopped to listen, but my cousin said, "Come on, let's go" and so I left with him. I dropped him off at his work, but I was very eager to come back and see these young girls. They were obviously prostitutes, like the ones you'd see on TV. They would ask if I wanted to have a fun time and if I wanted to see a girl. When I came back, there were three of them on the street.

I picked the prettiest one and I went over to her. She asked, "Do you want to see a girl?" The obvious answer is yes, but I wanted to know the cost, so I asked, "How much?" She said, "twenty dollars." This was in 1985 and twenty Australian dollars was about fifteen in US currency. She said I would have to pay ten dollars for the room, which totaled thirty dollars. We went upstairs, she gave the ten dollars to a guy for the room, and I went inside this small room with her. She asked me if this was my first time. I said, "Yeah." She said, "Just take off your clothes."

So, there I was. I had never been with a girl before, but I knew what it was like to take off my clothes because I've been to the nudist beach. I took off my clothes, and she had sex with me. I never realized at the time this simple act would lead to such a long and expensive addiction over almost my entire adult life.

At the time I was earning $230 a week from my job, $60 of which I could use as spending money. I thought it was absolutely amazing that I could afford two girls a week with that money. I found out the young girls were there in the afternoons, but not during the day.

I also learned some girls worked outside of strip joints and brothels. After I turned eighteen, I used to go there during the day. They had X-rated movies playing and stuff, sometimes strippers, and prostitutes used to come out into the audience and ask you if you wanted to go upstairs.

I quickly found out there were higher and higher grades of prostitutes. The lowest grade of prostitute was the streetwalker. A lot of the young girls, like the young girl that I saw, were just street kids that had left their parents' house due to abuse and were fresh to the streets. The girls that hired the rooms didn't have a pimp. They worked for themselves and didn't have to give anyone else their money. I used to like catching those girls, but they were just hard to find around my age. Most of the girls were under eighteen, more like sixteen or seventeen. If you are addicted to prostitutes you probably know this.

For women, Christians, or others curious about this book, this may seem strange. Why would a Christian man sleep with these young prostitutes? What? How could you do that? All I could say is, "I've got wounds inside of me. I don't know. I just have these crying needs."

Imagine you have a gushing wound on your arm. You could put a bandage on it, and it may stop the blood for a while, but not for long. If you're like me, pornography or seeing a prostitute is like putting a bandage on that gushing wound. It may help for a while, but eventually the blood will run again, and you've got to put on another bandage. The cycle continued.

I learned in one of these brothels that there was a thing called an escort. You could find them in the Yellow Pages of the phonebook. I don't know if you have that in America, but we used to have it before the internet. You could look under "escort agency" and find escorts in your suburb or one close by.

CHAPTER 6: THE ESCORT AGENCY

An escort agency is a place where you ring a number, and they'll send a girl to your place. You pay an hourly rate for the girl plus a certain amount for driving time. I found this one escort agency back in the late eighties. It was so expensive I could only afford one girl every two weeks. I think it was $200 for an hour back then—a far cry from twenty dollars. Plus, I think it was twenty dollars for the transport on top of that.

When I found this escort agency, they had fresh new girls every week. I found that I could just ring up on the night that I got the urge, how convenient. People who are sex addicts understand what an urge is. You get this insatiable desire to sin, and nothing can shut it down—a demonic influence in your life that you can't resist. So, you get on the phone and ring the escort agency. She'd tell you what girls were available, describe them to you, and then you pick which one you want. An hour later you get a knock on the door. If you aren't an addict or a victim, this may be foreign to you. But I want to tell my story so others will understand what this life is like.

I found the greatest thrill for me as an addict was opening the door to a total stranger and knowing that passing $220 dollars to her would allow you to take her clothes off and have sex. These girls from this escort agency were young, like eighteen, nineteen or twenty. A lot of them were university students putting themselves through college. They were like the "girls next door," if you have this term in America. These girls were very stunning. This particular escort agency was high-class, definitely not a lower rate company. The women were top-notch.

Proverbs 6:26 warns that a prostitute will reduce you to a loaf of bread. It's true. An addiction to escorts will make you very poor. You'll spend a lot of money. There's a breakfast cereal in Australia called "Weet-Bix." It's just made out of shredded wheat. I could live on Weet-Bix, milk, and sugar for five days. I could just eat this cereal as my only food. Today it costs about thirty dollars for five days, including the milk. So, I could spend all my money on escorts, and still live for five days cheaply. You shouldn't have to do that; you should be able to eat properly.

One day I was at home and got a call from this escort agency. This was before cell phones. The lady who called was from management and she said to me, "Matthew, you must be concerned why I'm ringing you, there's no problem".

I said, "Yeah."

She said, "Every time our girls go out, they come back and give us a report of how their date went, how their meeting went with the client, and you consistently get good reports from the girls. Many of the girls ask why you don't have them back. We understand that some clients like yourself like to see a new girl each time you ring. We're a large agency and we're always sending you a new girl because we know that you like that. Well, as a large agency we're constantly hiring new girls. You can understand it's a hard thing for a new girl to go and see her first client, or her first few clients. It's a very nerve-wracking thing for a girl. The reason I'm ringing you is because you've got a great reputation with our agency for treating the girls really nicely and you're a really nice client. I want to ask you if we could send our new girls to you once every two weeks when you get paid. Can we tell you the roster of our girls and when we have a new girl coming in, can we ring you and tell you which girls are starting that week, and can you arrange to meet one of these girls every two weeks when you get paid?"

I don't know how much you know about the sex industry. There are two types of clients—experienced and inexperienced. But just because you may be a regular client does not mean you have access to what the industry calls "fresh meat." Please excuse me for this term, but this is what they call it. Normally, a new client with an escort agency does not have access to these new girls. Only those with special authority get the fresh ones, like policemen, judges, politicians, or someone really connected.

A normal client like me does not get offers like this. So, when she asked me, you can be sure where all my money went every two weeks. She told me I could just show the girls what they need to do, how to please a client, what I liked, and give them any advice on how to be a good prostitute. So, I was getting sent young university students, attractive, stunning girls who'd never slept with a guy professionally before and I was the guy telling them what to do. It felt a tremendous amount of power. For those who know me you might be thinking, *"Matthew Robert Payne? I know him. How could he be doing this?"*

Once again, I'll get to the facts. I'm wounded, and I've got issues. But can you imagine how incredibly tempting this might be to a twenty-two-year-old, getting eighteen-, nineteen- or twenty-year-old girls who'd never had sex with anyone professionally before, and getting them on their first time? She reassured me that I would never have to see the same girl twice. The agency would find someone for their second time, and she guaranteed that. They start four girls every two weeks. So, I always have a choice of a new girl and I wouldn't have to see her ever again. I was voted one of their best clients. For over a year I saw new girls and introduced them to the prostitution business. But this also deeply cemented my sex addiction.

We believe certain lies about ourselves, whether you are a Christian or not. We might believe a lie like, "I'm not lovable, I'm not worthy, or I'm not good at this or that." We believe lies from the enemy, the devil, and this is how they get planted. And I believed a very bad one. I believed that since I was a good client, that I treated girls really well, and I had a good reputation with this agency, I was doing a good thing. But I was sexually abusing girls. What I thought was an awesome opportunity turned me into one of the most wicked people. I was introducing girls to a life of sex trafficking through the false pretense of being such a good client and showing them how nice things can be. And once I got a taste for high-class escorts it was very hard to go back to prostitutes in a brothel.

A brothel is different than an escort agency. They may have six girls there and each of the six girls comes and stands before you. You just pick which one you would like and then you take them upstairs. There's a certain rush when seeing several girls to choose from and picking the best one that you like. The girls have to parade themselves in front of a guy and it's very demeaning. Five out of the six don't get picked, but they've got to see all the clients as every man comes in. They have to go and put their best foot forward in the hopes that they are chosen.

They don't get paid an hourly rate while they're at the brothel. They only get paid per client, and they get 50% per client. So, you can see that they really want to impress the guys when they go into the room because they could stay there all night putting in eight or twelve hours and not get any money for it. The girls only get paid when they see a client. The sex industry has many victims.

CHAPTER 7: MY MARRIAGE, DIVORCE, AND REJECTION

At one stage, I joined Amway, which is a multi-level marketing business. I was fairly successful. But I was still addicted to prostitutes, so I had no money. For example, I was not able to fix my car for six months. I had to catch public transport everywhere because I was spending all my money on prostitutes. While I built my Amway business, I met a young girl that was very pretty. I was one of the leaders in the business. She introduced herself to me since she was part of my team.

She asked me if I could come and see her personally, but I told her to get someone else. She insisted that she wanted to see me. I thought to myself, *"that's pretty forceful."* So, I went and saw her and gave her some business training. I said, "I'm thinking of leaving the business because I think Jesus has told me that I'm not going to become an evangelist through this business. I think He wants to make me into an evangelist Himself, so I'm not the best person to be talking to you as I'm thinking of leaving the business."

I went to a conference where she also attended. She made sure she got my attention and wanted to talk to me. I said to her, "I've got to leave now. I've got a date tonight." She said, "You're going now? You're going to make me jealous." That's really forward behavior for a young girl. I thought that was great that she said that because I thought I'd follow that up and ask her out on a date, which I later did. I took her out for dinner, and we ended up in bed. In fact, I ended up spending so much time at her place that I said, "It would be best if I moved in with you," thinking this was really romantic of me. She said, "I'm not going to live with you unless you agree to marry me." I said, "That's fine." That was her proposal to me. Her name is Sharryn.

Sharryn had a controlling, Jezebel spirit. If you are not familiar with this term, the story of Jezebel can be found in 1 and 2 Kings in the Bible. Jezebel was a very seductive and controlling woman—the poster child, if you will, of such a person. I've also struggled with such an attitude of control, so I can't blame Sharryn. Sharryn said she was on the pill, but somehow got pregnant anyway. When she told me that she was pregnant, I no longer wanted to marry her.

My parents warned me that Sharryn's pregnancy by itself is not a good enough reason for us to get married. They were worried about me. Sharryn insisted that we were going to get married. My parents told me to let her have the child, and work on the relationship, and if the relationship goes well, then get married for sure. I told her what my parents told me. She said, "If you don't marry me, you'll never see me or the child again." So, I said, "Do you love me?" She said, "Of course I love you."

The marriage only lasted eighteen months. My addiction to prostitutes led me to many demons. On top of that, I now faced the pain from rejection, divorce, and the breakup of my family. The Lord spoke to me about my marriage. He said I still have unresolved pain and that I need more forgiveness over the whole situation. Most of my pain relates to the rejection of marrying this pretty wife, and then losing my son, as you will see in the next chapter. There's still a lot of work to be done in counseling. I still love Sharryn today, even though she caused me a lot of problems.

CHAPTER 8: LOSING MY SON

After our divorce, Sharryn started living with a guy, a preacher's son. They became engaged and she decided she was going to marry him. After their engagement, she said to me that I can't see my son anymore. I told her that I would fight her for custody in order to have access to my son.

Without going into details, Sharryn was into witchcraft. When I took her to court for custody of my son, she must have used witchcraft against me because I ended up in the psych ward. This led to a nervous breakdown and I developed a mental illness. I had this breakdown in the midst of this custody fight. I had never had mental problems prior to this.

When I got out of the psych ward, I told Sharryn I was going to take her to court again. She said, "You remember what happened the last time you tried that?" So I took the matter to Jesus. He said, "Don't fight over your son. I want you to move from Brisbane", a northern city in Australia. Jesus said, "I want you to move to Sydney, and I want you to let her new husband bring up your son."

As a father, this brought me unspeakable grief. My son is now twenty-seven, and it's been nineteen years since I've seen him. I only saw him once when he was twenty-two. He doesn't reach out to me or respond much to my emails. So, there's quite a bit of rejection there too. My wife rejected me, then my son. My heart is broken. Some people have known me for years and don't even known that I had a son. I have a very hard time talking about this to anyone.

CHAPTER 9: SUICIDAL THOUGHTS

When I broke up with my wife, I caught a train from Brisbane, a northern city, to Coffs Harbor where my parents lived. I'd lost my wife, and I was in the process of losing access to my son. At that time, I was only able to see my son two days every two weeks. This made me incredibly sad. My sister, Carmen, sat me down to talk to me.

During the conversation, I told Carmen that my wife Sharryn had been sexually abused by her stepfather. My sister had a list of twenty-five personality characteristics of those who were victims of sexual abuse. She said that she could see nine of these in Sharryn and asked me to sit down with the list and tell her how many I could see in Sharryn. I saw twelve. But as I went through the list, I noticed many of them also applied to me. Carmen said, "That's really interesting that you say Sharryn has twelve. This list has twenty-five, Matthew, and I've seen nine in Sharryn, but I've seen fifteen in you. Who abused you?"

This list was very comprehensive. If someone had more than six of them there was a good chance they were sexually abused. But if they had fifteen, they were definitely sexually abused. I'd lost my wife, my job, my child, and had nothing to hide anymore. My wife was my reason for living and my son gave me a lot of joy. I'd lost everything. When my sister asked who abused me, I opened up and told her all about the beach and what happened there.

I then realized that as a fourteen-your-old, I had been sexually abused and that I was a sexual abuse victim. I revealed my gay lifestyle and addiction to prostitutes before I met my wife. My sister never gave me a book on healing from sexual abuse or how to cope with it. She just opened this wound by explaining what happened to me but was unable to help me heal.

I was in the shower at my parent's place, feeling very broken. I was thinking about my hard life and how I didn't want to live anymore. I felt hopeless and had no answers. I finally decided in the shower that I might as well just end it by killing myself. Some people would say that Jesus is the prince of peace. But Satan can bring a sense of peace because once I made the decision to kill myself, a tremendous sense of relief came over me. I didn't stress about how I was going to do it; I just decided that I was going to.

As far as I know, my mother has only heard from God three times in her life. When she was outside the Holy Spirit told her, "Matthew's in danger." She immediately went to my younger brother, who was a counselor. She told him, "Get into the shower. Matthew's in trouble." I was just getting out of the shower when he came in. I was embarrassed because I was naked. I put a towel around myself and got angry at him for barging in like that.

He said, "What's going on?"

I said, "I've had enough."

He said to me, "I can understand you want to kill yourself."

My mother only told him that I was in trouble, and never mentioned that I was suicidal. So, I figure the Holy Spirit told him that. My brother said straight away, "I can understand you want to kill yourself. You've lost your wife and your child. Plus, we haven't been really friendly to you—haven't been a good family. I counsel at a drug rehabilitation farm. I've counseled guys that have been with me for a year who have overdosed within a week of leaving. I know that they didn't make a mistake with the heroin. I know that they gave themselves an overdose to commit suicide. Here I have you in front of me, and if I don't give you a reason to live, I know that you're going to kill yourself."

He continued, "You don't have to worry about Mum, Dad, your sister, brothers and your friends. You don't have to worry about them. I'll explain to them how you're feeling and how you are feeling depressed. I'll explain suicide to them and how dangerous it is, so you don't have to worry about killing yourself. I'll tide things over so that they won't call you weak or a coward. I'll make sure everything's right if you decide to kill yourself. I'll make sure everything's right with them." Then he started crying and said, "But I don't want to lose you. So, I've got to give you a reason to live."

He said, "You grew up with a violent father, a violent brother, and no real friends. You got married and your wife left you. You've lost your son, you've been sexually abused, you've slept with men, you've slept with prostitutes, and you've had addictions. Matthew, do you know all you need to do is get up and share your story? You don't even have to have answers for people. Do you know how many thousands of people would be in a better state if they heard your story? All you need to do is get up. I can see you in front of thousands of people one day just sharing your story. In that day, you don't even have to have the answers, just knowing what you've been through will be enough. If you can't get up for mum and dad and your sister and brothers, if you can't get up for your wife and your child or any of your friends, get up for those people." Somehow those words sunk in. I listened, and that's the reason for this book.

I once heard someone teach on suicide who said that it is important to give people permission to kill themselves, that it's important to accept they want to commit suicide and give them permission. Instead of telling them they can't kill themselves, what if you said, "That it's okay if you want to commit suicide, but can you do me a favor? When you decide to do it, can you come and see me one more time? I want to take you out for coffee to say goodbye" If you accept that they're going to do it and then offer them one more encounter with you before they do, you might save their life because you're not showing fear. The suicidal person needs others to validate the pain they are suffering, that they want to leave. If you can emphasize with them, it may take away the need to kill themselves. My younger brother gave me permission to kill myself, and then gave me a reason to live. That is why I am still here today.

Four times I have wanted to kill myself in my life and four times Jesus intervened by sending someone to speak to me and coach me back from the edge—just in the nick of time.

CHAPTER 10: SEEKING COUNSELING AND FINDING ISSUES

For years and years, I struggled with addictions to prostitutes and pornography. It really wore me down. I went to counseling one time with a ministry called Elijah House Ministries and they taught on repentance.

They said that in 1 Samuel 14 the prophet Samuel confronted King Saul for disobeying what he was told to do. Samuel specifically told Saul not to offer a sacrifice until he got there. But Saul, wanting to be a people pleaser, offered the sacrifice before Samuel arrived. Rather than taking responsibility for his actions and being repentant, Saul made excuses. But King David, on the other hand, was different. When the prophet Nathan confronted David for his sin with committing adultery with Bathsheba and murdering her husband to cover it up, he repented. The ministry gave our group a one-hour teaching on true repentance.

During our group discussion, I shared my addiction to prostitutes. The counselor said, "All I hear from you Matthew is boasting. You're not truly sorry. You actually think you're a good client. You actually think you treat the girls great. Until you can understand that you're abusing yourself, you're raping these girls, and you're abusing God, you will never be free. Until you can accept that and truly repent, you're never going to be free of this."

I went to my church the next week and publicly repented. The Holy Spirit told me to say out loud to the church that my righteousness is nothing but filthy rags. He wanted me to surrender my pride. After I repented in front of the church, I was free of my sexual addiction for six months. God sovereignly moved with his grace to set me free.

Shortly thereafter, I went on a ministry trip. A woman on the trip read a letter from a pedophile that had written to her. Something in that letter brought my lust back to life and my sex addiction returned. I have since tried repenting, but it has not worked. It was like I was back in the grips of a force greater than my willpower to resist.

However, when I was free, I got this sleep sickness. I would go to bed at 11 PM, wake up at 8 AM, and be very tired. I would go back to sleep, wake up at 11 AM, and still be tired. I would go back to sleep again, wake up at 2 PM, go back to sleep and still be too tired. Finally, I would wake up at 6 PM. Sometimes I would sleep twenty-one hours a day. Other days I would have to take sleeping pills. This roller coaster went on for four years. This sleep disorder began within a week of giving up prostitutes, so I believe there is somehow a connection.

I fell back into my addiction with prostitutes, which remains to this day. I tried more counseling with Elijah House Ministries. They talked about a situation where a mother, if mistreated by her husband, might subtly use her son as a pseudo spiritual husband. Because of the emotional disconnection with her husband, she might bond instead with a son, telling him her troubles and emotionally leaning on the son as a close friend. The one-hour video showed how destructive this can be and how badly this can injure her son.

At the end they said, "If this has happened to you, it will manifest itself in two ways. The son will have a mental illness, a major mental illness, like schizophrenia or bipolar. And the son will have a major sex addiction that can't be broken. I cried when I heard that because that's what my mother had done to me.

Here's another thing that's come out in counseling. I saw a vision of my mother coming home with the news that she was pregnant with me. My dad was very angry because he'd only planned on having two children. I was the third child. Elijah House Ministries talked about how a baby can be rejected in the womb, and how the baby can sense the rejection, if a father or mother doesn't want the child. So, before I was even born, I had rejection from my father. Then later I had this dysfunctional relationship with my mother, compounded by rejection from my wife and only child.

Also, when I was a young child, my father used to work a lot of overtime and he was always away. He left the house before I woke up in the morning and he came home after I'd gone to sleep. So, I would only see him one day a week. As a little child, I thought this was happening because my dad didn't love me, that he was rejecting me. I've got all these core issues that have to be fixed and even though I've tried counseling, I have yet to be healed from them.

CHAPTER 11: TRIED EVERYTHING. NO SUCCESS

I've gone to therapist after therapist, trying to get free of my addiction to pornography and prostitutes. I'm going to bring up this later, but in my time in churches, I hear so often how bad sexual sin is. Well, I can tell you from experience that it is very difficult to be free from the addictions to pornography and prostitutes. Yes, it is bad.

You feel so bound up with guilt, shame and condemnation. If you don't come before the Lord to be free, you just can't get anything done. You can't experience worship, you can't get close to God, and it really affects your intimacy with Jesus. Not only does the shame affect your walk with God, the guilt and the condemnation weigh you down. You constantly hear about people who fall into sexual sin. I'm guilty of committing adultery with prostitutes. All you ever hear about is how bad it is. I've tried and tried to get free. It's amazing how much people go on about those who fall like me.

Churches used to have free counseling. What ever happened to helping people who can't afford it? Elijah House Ministries wouldn't take my money. They do not charge for their services. But you have to pay for most counseling today. I'd gladly pay good money to find a therapist, deliverance minister—anyone, who can actually set me free.

I've been watching videos the last couple of days to find out what I may have to do to get free. I'm fifty-four, and thirty of them have been swallowed up by my addictions. And yet I've heard in the last couple of days things I have never heard before. Anyway, I have tried everything, yet no lasting success. I am fifty-three, turning fifty-four, and I'm still in bondage.

I want to say to you guys and girls out there who've got sex addictions that it's very hard to get free. It's very hard to break these addictions, and I understand. Here I am, a guy who's written over sixty books, 800 Christian articles, and done 3,000 Christian videos. I operate in a prophetic anointing and do prophecies for people and I still struggle. Here I am in Christian ministry. I'm addicted, and I'm guilty. I've hurt many people.

CHAPTER 12: FULL-BLOWN ESCORT ADDICTION

Some of the best girls not only work in escort agencies, but many of them freelance. They advertise for themselves and they run their own business. When I used to ring them up, I would ask them, "Do you kiss"? Rarely will a prostitute kiss, but I found this prostitute once in Brisbane years ago who kissed. I never used to see a prostitute twice. But this prostitute used to give me a massage and passionately kiss, so I kept seeing her.

One weekend she wasn't working, so I rang another prostitute and I asked her if she kissed. When she said she did I saw her. She kissed so passionately that I ended up getting engaged to that girl. It was a bit of a love story. You can read about her in my autobiography called *His Redeeming Love.*[1]

I won't go into it right now, but it's a really rare thing for a prostitute to kiss. There's an escort website in Sydney where girls freelance for themselves and run their own business. There is this service listed as "Deep French Kissing." You can look it up, and search for such a girl. All the girls that say they deep French kiss do passionately kiss, and I really like that. One of those escorts is $650 an hour.

---

[1] https://www.amazon.com/dp/B07H3M3NQV

Escorts can be very expensive. I had a full-blown escort addiction for years. With one particular girl I saw, we talked, we kissed, and we had sex. I'll tell you another thing about escorts, which people addicted to prostitutes would know. Not only do these girls rarely kiss, but they also rarely have a sexual climax. Rarely will a prostitute ever orgasm. Most prostitutes will make noises like they are, but they're faking it. I can't speak for every guy because I'm not every guy, but I can tell when a girl is having a real orgasm or not.

Anyway, I had this girl. Her escort name was Hailey. She defied the odds when it came to escorts enjoying themselves. I booked her again and she knew I was a Christian. The next time I was with her she said, "Do you like this singer?" It was Kim Walker-Smith from the band Jesus Culture. I said "Yeah." She said, "I've got some songs on an album that she produced. Can I sing them to you?" The songs were playing on her iPhone. The music played out loud and she sang three of Kim's songs; she was really worshiping. She's a twenty-three-year-old stunning blonde and she's singing her heart out, worshiping in bed naked with me. I just couldn't sleep with her after that. If you are interested in knowing the songs, you can look up Kim Walker-Smith. The three songs are, "Just One Touch", "On My Side", and "You Define Me".

In the song "You Define Me", Kim was singing to the Lord and it was though this prostitute was genuinely singing this to the Lord in bed with me. Here are some of the lyrics:

Only Your words define me

You tell me who I am

Only Your love can hold me

You make me who I am

You define me, You define me

It's an amazing song. I decided that I couldn't see her for sex anymore, something I have never done before. I texted her after this asking "Do you ever meet just for coffee"? She said, "Yeah." I asked how much it would be and she said it was $250 for an hour." I said "Well, that's a third of the price. That's a good deal." I raced to meet her for coffee, and we talked for an hour. I found that I didn't need to have sex. I just needed someone to talk to. I thought, *"well, this will be the answer. I'll just pay to meet for coffee and I'll see her every month"*. I live on a mental health disability pension. I also have money from my prophetic ministry, but I don't use that to pay for the girls.

I thought I could just have her as a friend like this, but she never committed to seeing me for coffee again. She couldn't understand why I had seen her for sex twice, why I had seen her for coffee once, and only wanted to see her for coffee again from then on. We exchanged a few emails since then and she was courteous, but we never met or spoke again. I have a soft heart and my heart was taken with this worshipping escort. After her, I took a few escorts out for coffee, but it was playing with fire. I eventually succumbed to having sex with them.

I had a full-blown escort addiction. I have fallen for three escorts in my life. I tend to fall for most of the girls that I see more than once. One time, one of the prostitutes fell in love with me also. That story can also be found in my book *His Redeeming Love.* [2]

---

[2] https://www.amazon.com/dp/B07H3M3NQV

CHAPTER 13: A FULL-BLOWN PORN ADDICITON

When you are addicted to prostitutes and you have the money to see a one, when the urge comes on, there really is nothing that can stop you. There's a demonic influence in your life. When you have the money to see a prostitute, when that urge comes on to see a woman, the strength of the temptation is like a ten out of ten. When you've got a demon that is very difficult to resist, well, it's like it owns you. When you've broken the addiction, like I've broken it for six months twice before, when the temptation comes on, the strength of the temptation is only one out of ten. So, you can easily say no to it. But when you've got the full-blown addiction, when the temptation comes, it's full on.

One of the ways I found to keep from spending so much money on prostitutes when the urge comes on is to masturbate to pornography. That way, when I run myself out of sperm, I wouldn't be wasting my money on a prostitute so soon. What a sad state to be in—avoiding one sin only to indulge in another.

I recently listened to a guy's teaching about habitual addictions. Our neural pathways in our mind become programmed for the addiction. So, to break it, the neural pathways have to be rewritten. This is not an easy fix. It's not just saying a simple prayer of repentance—trust me. I've had full-blown addictions to escorts and prostitutes. I have had many times when I have lasted a week or two and thought I was finally free. I was happy, and then came a powerful temptation, and the freedom that I was enjoyed ended.

Pornography has many terrible effects on your brain and your attitude toward women. It is tough having this addiction. It's very bad; I can tell you quite plainly.

CHAPTER 14: CONFESSING SINS IN MY BOOKS

If you've ever read one of my books, you'll notice that I'm very open and transparent about my sin life in my books. I often mention my addiction to pornography and prostitutes and writing about it is one of the ways I've tried to get free. James 5:16 says,

> "Build your faith by surrounding yourself with Christians you trust and who love and encourage you. Regularly confess your sins to one another. Pray for each other. Healing and forgiveness will naturally flow. Anyone *who lives the way God wants* and who learns to *pray effectively,* consistently, and persistently, as a matter of lifestyle, will *produce massive, maximum results.*"

Because of this verse, I decided to keep these sins out in the open and not try to hide them. Secrecy maintains their power over you. I know that producing this book takes power away from the enemy, the devil, I mean. I know that he's not happy about this book because it's going to produce good fruit. I have experienced untold shame since starting this book, not to mention the temptations have really ramped up.

There's been quite a bit of warfare in getting this book published. By warfare, I mean demonic attacks on my thinking, and throwing temptations my way. I have constantly confessed my sins in my books about my struggles with these sins. I want you to know that it'll do you good if you're reading this book to confess your sins to someone like James 5:16 says above.

I'm here saying to you that I haven't got answers yet. But I'm thinking that part of my answer is to go back and get counseling. One guy who shared a video I watched said that he needed community, and he found it in "Sex Addicts Anonymous". He needed that community, and he needed a sponsor to get free to rewrite his pathways in his mind. So, my next step is to join a group for sex addicts. He is a pastor who was addicted to porn and prostitutes even though he was married. The name of the YouTube video is *A Pastor's Struggle with Pornography and Prostitutes—Gary Wilkerson Podcast—035.* [3] I recommend you watch it. He does a much better job than me in explaining this struggle.

He says one of the most common misconceptions is that you'll be able to solve it yourself and one day God will just take it away. He said that he had times of "sobriety", but whenever pressure came into his life, he went back to his addiction. So, you want to make a permanent break. You don't want to be free for say three months and then fall back again.

When I was free from my addictions for six months recently in the last year, I thought that I was finally free. I did a seventeen-minute video about this. I was so happy. 4,000 people have watched that video and so many people have commented on it.

---

[3] Accessible via https://www.youtube.com/watch?v=tjCRR2YT7_I

It's been so popular and helped a lot of people. However, I later fell back into it and I felt so ashamed. I want to tell you guys it's such a lonely, sad state to be in. If you can find people, if you can go to Sex Addicts Anonymous, if you can find people to relate to and to talk honestly with no holds barred, I am sure it will be helpful.

Talk about your sin, talk openly about your problems. You're going to find relief and camaraderie in other men and other addicts. I was too proud. I never wanted to be part of one of these groups, thinking that I've got a disease, that I'm a victim, and that I'm hopeless. I just wanted to fix it myself. Jesus has brought me full circle. He's humbled me a lot. My sin has humbled me, and I've had enough.

It seems that if I am ever going to be free of this, I need to do more than confess my sin in the books that I write. I have to put more work into conquering this thing. Sure, my readers can pray for me, but they are helpless to stop me. I'm the one that has to say, No." And I owe it to the world to get free from this.

CHAPTER 15: A SIX-MONTH RELIEF FROM MY SIN

As I shared earlier, years ago I confessed in church that my righteousness is as filthy rags. That set me free for six months. But then I heard that pedophile's letter, and that sent me back into my addictions. Before the letter, during those six months the temptations were on a scale of one out of ten. But after the letter, it was like something grabbed a hold of me and pulled me down and I was unable to resist. That six-month relief did have many benefits though. I thought I was finally free. It's hard not to get prideful when you get free; you start boasting and you start being really happy.

If you're reading this and you're not a sex addict because you want to find out information, can you imagine living your Christian life always sinning? Where you're always feeling condemned with guilt and shame, where you constantly have to get your peace back with God?

The pastor in the above-quoted video spoke of these times of reprieve that we have before our addiction is finally gone. I hope that as I share my life with you, if you are suffering with addictions, my words bring you some encouragement, at least to know that you are not alone. Whilst getting free for a few weeks or a few months is commendable, we all want permanent and lasting freedom.

CHAPTER 16: FALLING BACK INTO SIN

Recently, when I was free for six months, it was a tremendous relief—it was amazing. My brother actually came to stay at my house. He too had an addiction to pornography and prostitutes. When he stayed at my house, he got free of the sin. It was like there was a presence in my house that got him free too. I was really happy for that six months; it was a really happy time in my Christian life.

But falling back into sin was so depressing, so sad for me. I don't know how you feel, or how many pastors or people in ministry reading this book feel. But when you've got these sins in your life and you can't get free, it's like the sin gains strength knowing you can't conquer it. Like it has a personality of its own. When you've got these sins in your life and you can't conquer it, it just breaks your heart. It just makes you feel worthless; it makes you feel hopeless. But when you finally admit that you can't conquer it and you need help, I think you're on your way to freedom.

It is a sad thing that your self-esteem and self-worth can come down to whether or not you are sinning. This is a sad reality of the Christian church that we are all part of. It is such a hard cross to bear being a sinner.

CHAPTER 17: THREE STAGES OF MY LIFE, MY MOTHER SAYS

My mother died in August 2019. As I write this, it has been eighteen months. I speak to my mother who is now in Heaven; I can speak to her anytime I choose. I'll explain more on how it is that I can talk to people in Heaven at the end of this chapter.

My mother had this long conversation with me once and said my life would be in three stages. She said the first stage was producing my first fifty-five books, and that I would also have a second and third stage.

Now I'm entering into the second stage, which is a stage of healing and rest. I used to strive a lot, always doing things to impress God, and doing things to make myself feel good. She said that when I stop writing so many books and I have a time of healing and rest, Jesus is going to teach me how to move out of striving and live from a place of rest.

She said the third stage in my life will begin when I am discovered; I'm going to be popular in the world. At that stage I'll have all these books behind me, and it will go really well. She told me clearly that I had three stages and I'm now in this middle stage of rest and healing. I've realized that no one wants to get healed more than me. This insight from my mother has brought me a lot of peace.

I remember when my wife first left me. I went to this Pentecostal church and went to a men's camp. It was a fellowship camp and the Pentecostal minister said he was going to prophesy—that he would do prophecies for each one of us. I didn't know what prophecy was because I was a Baptist. They do not teach on or operate in the gift of prophecy. I learned later though that the gift of prophecy is certainly for today. For example, Ephesians 4:11-12 says, "Speaking of gifts, in the Church, some are gifted to be apostles, some prophets, some evangelists, and some pastors and teachers—all by God's choosing. Their purpose is to fully train and equip the saints to serve others effectively, to build up the Body of Christ."

First Corinthians 14:1-5 goes further:

> "Your ultimate goal is love. But trust me, be passionate to have and develop spiritual gifts, *especially* the gift of prophecy. When you hear someone speaking in tongues you know that no one knows what they are saying (unless there is someone there with the gift to interpret tongues) because tongues is directed to God. Indeed, the Holy Spirit is communicating mysteries. But prophecy is for us, to help us grow in the faith, and to bring encouragement and comfort. When you pray in tongues, your spirit is strengthened. But when someone prophesies, the whole Church benefits. Now understand this: I do want all of you to be able to at least pray in tongues, but truth be told, I would rather you prophesy. Someone who prophesies is

much more useful than one who can speak in tongues, unless of course, there is someone there to interpret. That way the whole church can gain from it."

The minister said to us, "I'm going to pray for you and at a certain time in the prayer, Jesus is going to speak to you through me. When He begins speaking, I'll say, 'thus saith the Lord', and then Jesus will speak. Jesus has been speaking to me all my life."

When I was about twenty-six, I learned how to hear from Jesus. So, I was amazed when he said that he has been hearing from Jesus his whole life. As I shared earlier, Jesus had spoken to me in verses and lyrics from songs before, and I had a good relationship with Him. I was impressed that the speaker could hear from Jesus too.

The minister came over to me and said, "Thus saith the Lord. You're really in a dark tunnel at the moment, and you can't see that there's going to be any light at the end of the tunnel. You don't even know if there's even going to be light at the end of the tunnel."

My wife had just left me, and she had an affair with another man. She had another boyfriend, and I wanted her to break up with him and come back to me. I lost custody of my son and I was only seeing him every two weeks. It was a very dark time. I really loved my wife, and I was pining for her. I wanted her back and I was really depressed. It was a very dark tunnel.

He continued, "There's going to be light and one day you're going to come out of the tunnel. God is going to heal you and then He's going to raise you up into ministry. And just as Billy

Graham was known throughout the world, so shall your name be."

About a year ago, I received another prophecy. It read, "Jesus says, 'You've just come out of the tunnel.'" It didn't mean anything to the person who gave me this prophecy, but it meant a lot to me because that meant I was entering into this next stage of my life. At the end of that prophecy, he said "You're going to be healed and then God's going to raise you up in the ministry."

Well, I've been trying to promote myself into the ministry by writing these books, doing videos, and writing articles. I've always known that I've got to be healed. I've tried, and I've tried—no one's tried harder than me. I've gone from counselor to counselor really trying to be healed. Along the way I realized that I had to be humbled. I had to reach a stage where I'll actually go to Sex Addicts Anonymous. Maybe for you it may take a year or two, maybe five, until you are humble enough to reach out for help. For me, I'm never going to get to stage three until I heal.

Part of my healing journey is producing this book. Part of my healing was to obey the Holy Spirit and confess all this and say, "Hey, I'm this guy that's written over sixty books, but I'm just a broken individual." Everything I say in my books is true. I encourage you to follow Jesus and obey Him as I do no matter what He tells you to do. Despite my sexual sin, I have this tremendous intimate relationship with Jesus. But I have to reach this third stage. I have to finish my healing; I have to be healed. And then God's going to raise me up into the ministry of helping others

You may be wondering what I meant when I said I have conversations with my mother after she died. Well, let me explain. On my thirtieth birthday, Jesus said to me, "You never ask Me for anything. I want you to ask me for something. I'm going to answer your prayer." "How much time do I have to decide?" I asked. Jesus said, "Take as much time as you want."

As I pondered this, a scripture verse came to mind from Acts 2:17:

> "'In the last days,' God says,
>
> 'I will pour out my Spirit upon all people.
>
> Your sons and daughters will prophesy.
>
> Your young men will see visions,
>
> and your old men will dream dreams.'" (NLT)

So, after I thought about it, I said to Jesus, "I want prophetic dreams and visions." Shortly thereafter, Jesus introduced me to Mary Magdalene in a vision. Since then, I have had many conversations with her. In fact, I have met many other saints from Heaven. I have published several books on Amazon detailing those conversations, including Kind David, the Apostle Paul, Enoch, Elijah, and many more. I have also interviewed other contemporary saints in Heaven including Michael Jackson and Princess Diana, to name a few.

In case you do not know, while Jesus is the center piece, the Holy Spirit is essentially the social coordinator of Heaven. He is in charge of these visits and conversations. I do not initiate these encounters. And even if I did, the saints only say what the Holy Spirit has for me at that moment.

Some people have criticized me as being a necromancer, or someone who talks to the dead. I am not talking to evil spirits, or spirits from Hell. God considers saints in Heaven as alive and not dead. In Luke 20:37-38 Jesus said, "Long after Abraham, Isaac, and Jacob had died, he [Moses] referred to the Lord as 'the God of Abraham, the God of Isaac, and the God of Jacob.' So, he is the God of the living, not the dead, for they are all alive to him." (NLT)

If you still think that talking to people who have died but are in Heaven is still necromancy, then is Jesus guilty of that too? Matthew 17:1-3 records an encounter where Jesus talked with Moses and Elijah well after, of course, both of them had died: "Six days later Jesus took Peter and the two brothers, James and John, and led them up a high mountain to be alone. As the men watched, Jesus' appearance was transformed so that his face shone like the sun, and his clothes became as white as light. Suddenly, Moses and Elijah appeared and began talking with Jesus." (NLT) No, Jesus is not guilty of necromancy, and neither am I.

Ephesians 2:6 says, "For he raised us from the dead along with Christ and seated us with him in the heavenly realms because we are united with Christ Jesus." (NLT) In a nutshell, we were given an all-access pass to Heaven the moment we invited Jesus into our hearts when we believed the Gospel of salvation. You can have encounters like this too.

Some Christian leaders teach against the supernatural workings of the Holy Spirit. They falsely spread rumors and fear discouraging Christians from operating in the supernatural. But Jesus is very clear that we should have no such fear of asking God for the gifts and manifestations of the Holy Spirit. In Luke 11:11–13, Jesus said:

> "Which of you parents, if your child asked you for a sandwich, would give them a rock? Or if they asked for a snack, would you give them a snake? Or if they asked you for a treat, would you give them poison? If you parent, though you are bad compared to God, know how to give good gifts to your children when they ask and not harm them, how much more will your Heavenly Father do the same? He will give the Holy Spirit to those who continually ask Him and not bring them any harm." (Dundy Style Version)

What Jesus is basically saying is that opening yourself up to the supernatural as directed by the Holy Spirit will not result in you getting a demon instead, as some Christian leaders falsely teach. Truth be told, inciting this fear not only keeps Christians from being much more effective in prayer and healing, but this comes dangerously close to blasphemy of the Holy Spirit, which is not a forgivable sin.

I do not know why Jesus gave me the ability to communicate and basically have two-way conversations with Him and with saints in Heaven. When I asked for visions and dreams, I never expected it to turn out this way. I am most underserving. I can identify with the Apostle Paul in 1 Timothy 1:15-16, "This is a trustworthy saying, and everyone should accept it: "Christ Jesus came into the world to save sinners" — and I am the worst of them all. But God had mercy on me so that Christ Jesus could use me as a prime example of his great patience with even the worst sinners. Then others will realize that they, too, can believe in him and receive eternal life." (NLT)

With what I have shared so far as to my moral failures and sin life, it should be no surprise to you that God did not give me these gifts, or my gift of prophecy, because I am anyone special. Believe me I am not. Nonetheless, these gifts are a huge part of my life, not the least of which are the thousands and thousands of prophecies I have given people over the years.

I know this was a bit long, but I have never explained how I am able to have two-way conversations with saints in Heaven in any of my books or videos before.

CHAPTER 18: PROBLEMS WITH HIDDEN SIN IN THE CHURCH

Back in 2014, more than half of Christian men admitted to watching pornography.[4] A more recent study actually shows "68% of church-going men and over 50% of pastors view porn on a regular basis. Of young Christian adults eighteen to twenty-four years old, 76% actively search for porn."[5]

I've been so frank with my sin to talk about this. If over two thirds of men in the church have got a problem with pornography, then that is huge. A 2007 survey in the UK found "one in five men in the UK has enlisted the services of a sex worker."[6] If even half of men in the church are addicted to porn, then when you are raising your hands to worship, either the guy on your left or guy one on the right is one of them. If the church holds 300 adults in a service, 150 men, then seventy-five of them are addicted to porn, and there's a good chance some of them on stage are too.

James 5:16 says,

> "Build your faith by surrounding yourself with Christians you trust and who love and encourage you. Regularly

---

[4] https://www.washingtontimes.com/news/2014/aug/24/more-than-half-of-christian-men-admit-to-watching-/. Last accessed March 24th, 2021.

[5] https://conquerseries.com/15-mind-blowing-statistics-about-pornography-and-the-church/. Last accessed March 24th, 2021.

[6] https://www.nydailynews.com/life-style/guy-prostitute-article-1.290486. Last accessed March 24th, 2021.

confess your sins to one another. Pray for each other. Healing and forgiveness will naturally flow. Anyone *who lives the way God wants* and who learns to *pray effectively, consistently, and persistently,* as a matter of lifestyle, will *produce massive, maximum results.*"

The sad fact of the matter is very few if any in the ministry are forthcoming about sex addiction. I was really blessed by seeing this pastor make the video I mentioned before.[7] Watching his video and his admission that he was addicted to prostitutes and porn was very helpful to me.

Recently we've heard that Ravi Zacharias, a world-famous Christian evangelist, has been exposed for seeing all these massage therapists and having a massive sex addiction.[8] The whole world's gone crazy over it. The whole Christian church is throwing stones at him, but my question is why does such a powerful man of God get trapped in a sin like that, and why aren't there people that he can talk to and get free of it?

See, here's the problem. You can't confess your sin in the church, and that shouldn't be the case. You should be able to confess your sins and get free of them. You should be able to have people that can walk with you and support you and understand you.

I shared with a former pastor of mine that I was going to do this book called *Stop Throwing Stones* and he mentioned Ravi's situation. He said it is such a shame that Ravi had no one to confide in. He couldn't get free—that he was stuck in this sin.

---

[7] Accessible via https://www.youtube.com/watch?v=tjCRR2YT7_I
[8] https://reformationcharlotte.org/2021/02/12/ravi-zacharias-sexual-misconduct-report-released-its-worse-than-we-thought/. Last accessed March 24th, 2021.

Some people are saying Ravi is in hell. Well, he's in heaven because I have already spoken to him. One of the prophets I follow accused Ravi of being a false prophet and false teacher. He said Ravi was a wolf in sheep's clothing. But I say he was still a Christian and he was a broken man. We just don't know the whole story.

What happens to all the broken men and the broken women in church? The problem is there's hidden sin in the church. People come to church and you ask them how they are, and they say, "Yeah I'm fine," but the night before they may have been masturbating to porn. There are so many problems, so many problems with an addiction to porn. It makes you look at women as objects; it changes your view of them. Your eyes undress them. You think women are meat. You think women can be used and it lowers your opinion of them. There are so many things wrong with pornography—bad behavior, bad thoughts, and bad mind concepts. So, if 50% of the men in church are addicted to porn, then we've got a big problem. It's not just single men as a lot of married men have the same issue. You may be wondering as a woman or as a wife if your man addicted to porn. If he is, how is he going to get free? The video I shared earlier will help you find answers.

Your man needs to work on himself if he's addicted to porn. He's got work to do if he's addicted to prostitutes. The problem has to get fixed. And it's not going to go away on its own. The video describes that, and I can verify this from personal experience. I thought it was going to go away by itself when I was free of it for six months; it just happened. The neural pathways for those six months—had they been reprogrammed, and then switched back to the old way. I don't know what happened. I was supernaturally delivered by the grace of God.

Here's something I want to share with you. If nothing you've ever tried has worked and you can't get free in your own power, you need the grace of God to set you free. If, for whatever reason, the grace of God isn't being given to you, if God isn't giving you the power to overcome, who's responsible? If you need a sovereign act of grace to stop, are you really responsible if you can't?

This is what I find with the Christian church—they are all too eager to throw stones. Remember the woman caught in adultery in John 8:1-11? The accusers all surrounded her to stone her. I heard someone describe what being stoned was like. It breaks your body into all sorts of pieces internally. Parts of your body, your internal organs, start to break down. You bleed from the inside out. It's just a horrific death. Well, that's what they were going to do to this woman. Jesus bent down and started writing in the sand. I personally believe that what He was writing in the sand was the sins of those waiting to stone her. And when they read them, they all walked away. When Jesus stood back up, only the woman was left. He said to her, "Where are your accusers? Didn't even one of them condemn you?" "No, Lord," she said. And Jesus said, "Neither do I. Go and sin no more." (John 8:10-11. NLT)

Many people focus on that last part, "Go and sin no more." But the first part brought healing to her heart: "Neither do I condemn you." Those words were spoken from the most righteous man in Israel, a rabbi, saying to her she wasn't condemned.

When you're stuck in sin, which she was as she was caught in adultery, you think you're worthless. His words "Neither do I condemn you" healed her, but Christians too often stress the second part "Go and sin no more." They say you can be forgiven, but you've got to stop sinning. Those who stress "Go and sin no more," but do not offer forgiveness, do not bring healing—only condemnation. So, some judgmental Christians use the phrase, "Go and sin no more" like the stones the Jews were going to kill the woman caught in adultery. Do you realize how this feels to someone who can't seem to get free from the sin that holds them?

One of the things that keeps you locked in sin are these cyclical bondages. Each time you get free but then fall back into sin, it gets worse. Each time you fall, your neural pathways to shame, guilt and condemnation get stronger. The more worthless you feel, the less you can resist temptations. If the healing and freedom are not permanent, it becomes more and more difficult to get free the next time. So, we all need Jesus to say, "You're forgiven."

Honestly, I'm telling people that want to judge me and judge people, like Ravi Zacharias, that they are throwing stones. He is guilty but the same Messiah would have picked him up, and He would have turned around to the people and said, "You without sin, throw the first stone." And is there really one of you reading this who is without sin? Can you honestly say you are living a sinless life right now?

I've met two apostles in the past who said they weren't sinning anymore. But both apostles admitted that they had sinned before. Is there anyone sinless? Do you qualify to cast a stone because you are without sin? This book is about getting the church to stop throwing stones. And those who throw stones do not even admit their own sin. They keep them hidden.

Sin holds its power as long as it remains a secret. Part of my healing process is writing this book—exposing, rather than hiding, my sins. I know I also need to chase down a sex addict group, and God's going to probably open a way for me to heal there as well. But first, I had to go through this door of obedience, to write this book, and sharing my heart with you.

The main issue here is that we live in a culture where there's no one safe to confess our sins to. If over half of men are addicted to pornography, who are they going to turn to? Have they told anyone? What if you are a worship leader? Will their church be open to them confessing that they masturbate to porn three times a week? Who are they going to tell? If you have no one safe to go to for support and encouragement, how will they hear Jesus say, "neither do I condemn you"? How will they ever get free? That is the issue, folks.

While I am unknown, while I have no reputation, I'm writing this book. One day I believe I will be a famous evangelist. I will have a big name and these sins will be a thing of the past—that third stage in my life my mother told me about. My past won't affect me because I will have already brought it out into the open. When I share my story with those struggling with these same addictions, people will respect the fact that I already laid down the foundation of honest and open confession which led to my healing. People will be able to say, "If you read Matthew's books from this date to this date, you will read how he very candidly shares his struggles. He did not hide them." Hopefully I will not fall again in the future, but if I did, people will be much more understanding than if I tried to keep them a secret. Folks, we have a culture of sin, hidden sin, and we have a culture of abusers. This situation is getting worse because the church does not want to deal with it.

We can't tell anyone because people throw stones—people judge. Another reason why sin is so rampant in church leadership is that we put these people on pedestals. We have our own "Hollywood" when it comes to the ministry. It's a natural thing to want heroes, but what happens if you are one of those on a pedestal? Who are they going to go to if they have an issue? How could Ravi share with someone that he's regularly sexually abusing girls? Where is someone so famous like him going to turn for help that won't punish him and remove him from ministry?

Another famous evangelist is Todd Bentley. He was exposed two years ago for sexually abusing his staff, apparently for many years. He had one of the most powerful ministries in the world. Where can someone on such a pedestal go to confess and get help? To someone on his staff? How can he reach out to another leader and say, "I've got this issue on abusing my interns"? He would have been taken out of ministry and he'd lose everything that's important to him! Because there's such a consequence to them openly confessing their sin, they never do it. Therein lies the problem. There's this major problem with hidden sin in churches. While we have a culture of wearing faces and putting our best foot forward and not being honest with one another, the hidden sins are not dealt with and so many people are going to remain in bondage.

Many Christians simply aren't honest people. They just don't walk in truth. You can get an honest conversation about addiction to prostitutes in the pub within five minutes with a stranger. You can say, "I saw a prostitute last night and, geez, she's a great kisser." Right away the guy's talking to you. You can't say that in a church. You can't lean aside with a cup of coffee after church and say the same thing. Of course, if you did, they would take you to the pastor and you'd get kicked out of the church. But here's the problem guys. What if the pastor has the same problem and he's hiding it?

If he tells his wife, he loses his marriage. If he tells the elders, he loses his job. Is he going to confide in the worship leader? Someone has to come forward. Someone has to make a video or write a book. It's not until the pastors who are hiding this sin come forward that those under them can find freedom themselves. Change has to start somewhere. When enough people, leaders, come forward and live in the light, and not hide their sin in darkness, others will find the courage to do the same. Someone has to say, "I've got that problem. Then someone else can admit, "I've got that problem too." You will find this freedom in Alcoholics Anonymous, or Sex Addicts Anonymous. Again, James 5:16 says we are to build our faith by surrounding ourselves with Christians we trust and who love and encourage us. We are to regularly confess our sins to one another and pray for each other. Healing and forgiveness will naturally flow. What church do you know of that models such basic openness? I haven't found one.

On the topic of suicide, there have been four times in my life that I was going to kill myself, and four times Jesus intervened by sending someone to save my life. Just mentioning suicide, just mentioning that I've been suicidal, four times in fact, helps those who may be struggling with depression and suicide. Just the fact of mentioning that I was suicidal, brings comfort to so many thousands of people. Mentioning that I was sexually molested, sexually abused on a beach, also brings comfort to so many people. Mentioning that I've been homosexual and have done homosexual acts also brings comfort. Telling people that I'm addicted to prostitutes and I really enjoyed some encounters with some escorts brings comfort to people. It's called living in the light.

First John 1:5-9 says it well:

> "Here is the message we heard from Him and want to pass on to you—God is light. There is no darkness in Him at all. If we say we are Christians but keep on living in the dark, our life is nothing but a big lie—we're not telling the truth. On the other hand, if we continually walk in the light, just like Jesus does, then we are fellow Christians, and the blood of Jesus Christ His Son will continually cleanse us from each and every sin. If we refuse to admit we are sinners, we are only fooling ourselves—there's no truth inside us. When God exposes our sin, if we agree and confess our sins to Him when He brings them to light, He is faithful and will do the right thing and forgive our sins because of Christ's sacrifice. Plus, He will keep on cleansing us from all aspects of our sin."

We can't get free by hiding our sin. We have to find a way to do what James says to do. Since prostitutes are so expensive, if I tell people the only way I save money is masturbating, some men will understand that. But why does it take me to do this? Why out of all the Christians in the world, why out of all the preachers in the world, and all the therapists in the world, why has the Holy Spirit told me to write this book to say that? This is really embarrassing for me. Although it's helpful for me, I know that there must be other reasons that the Holy Spirit has me doing this. The church just hides its sin. Well, I've got nothing to lose guys. I'm not getting invited to speak in churches. I'm not preaching, and I haven't got an international ministry.

But I can tell you that in five years' time, if I'm traveling the world as an evangelist, this book's going to have power. People from all walks of life are going to come and listen to me because they know I'm authentic. Because when I was still struggling with issues, when very few people knew me, I was admitting my problems. So, here I am guys. I'm asking for help. If you are a therapist and can help me, please get in touch because I want it.

We can't get free of this pain until the pain is healed. On one occasion, I went to a massage parlor where they trafficked women. When I went in, the three girls that came into the room were shivering in the corner in fear. I knew right away that these girls had had their passports stolen and were now getting forced to do this. I walked out of there. I didn't want any part of that. Unlike America, prostitution is legal in Australia. Every woman that has been part of my addiction has not been a slave. They earn about 50% from the sales.

Don't get me wrong. This does not relieve me of my guilt. But as far as I know, I have not slept with a woman who was being forced to do it. No little six-year-old girl says to her dad "When I grow up, I want to be an escort." Girls don't think in high school that when they grow up, they want to become an escort, even if they make good money doing it. Girls don't go to vocational training on how to become an escort. No girl decides that, so every girl in the sex industry, every woman working in the sex industry, is a victim.

I fully embrace the fact, and I'll say here, that I'm partly to blame for their victimization. But, I'm appealing to you. I'm a victim too. And I want to be healed and want this fixed. I have already confessed quite clearly that I felt like the king of the world when that escort agency asked me to help bring the new girls into the industry—yes, to victimize them.

I freely admit that I was doing a bad thing there. I freely admitted in the counseling session at Elijah House Ministry that I was boasting about it. You may think I am bragging about my sexually addictive lifestyle. Nothing could be further from the truth. I am only being this open to help with my repentance. It may seem I am making excuses all over the place and that I am such an evil person. You can throw stones at me all you want because that seems the only answer Christians have right now.

So, pick up your stones. But who's ever going to speak up for the victims? Who's going to ever speak for the abusers? Jesus loves the abusers. Jesus came to set the captives free and there's no more of a captive than someone who's abusing.

This has been a hard book to produce. I've had a lot of warfare around this book. My flesh didn't want to do it. This is a real act of obedience to God. Feel free to throw stones at me. But my question to you is, "Have you got the answers"? Because if you do, I'd love it, really love it.

CHAPTER 19: STOP THROWING STONES

I have an angel that helps me write. You may wonder how I could ever minister with angels and have angels around me since I've had such bad addictions. But I've got a scribe angel, which is an angel that helps me write and make videos. She gave me the title to this book, *Stop Throwing Stones. The Anatomy of a Christian Prophet's Sex Addiction.* She gave me the title and the subtitles, the chapters for this book, and she has given me the courage to share these words with you. I explained earlier how I began to work with saints in Heaven. Well, that includes angels too.

In the church, we need to stop throwing stones. People have to stop hiding their sins in the church. Maybe you could share this book with your pastor. If he is seeing prostitutes or knows of someone else who is, or has a porn addiction, this book may help. If you're reading this and you're using pornography, or you are addicted to prostitutes, tell someone this week.

One way you could tell them is "I want you to read this book and I've got something to tell you." The church has got to stop throwing stones because Jesus didn't throw a stone at the woman caught in adultery as I shared earlier. And He was without sin, so He qualified. Do you hear Jesus saying to you, "Neither do I condemn you?"

I was in a dirty massage parlor one time where they do a massage like Ravi's sin. They give you a massage and then they masturbate you, give you hand relief. I had just left one of those parlors and walked down the street filled with guilt and condemnation, feeling really bad. About two minutes later I passed a little Asian girl, who was about six. I said to Jesus, "She's really innocent." Jesus said, "That's how I see you, you're really innocent too."

That statement stopped me in my tracks. I had just had a dirty massage and hadn't confessed that sin to Jesus yet. You have no idea how much that statement impacted me. As I shared earlier, the cycle of guilt, shame and condemnation further solidifies the power sin has over you. And Christians who judge me and throw stones only make it worse. If I only see myself as a horrible sinner, then how is my self esteem ever going to break out of this prison? When Jesus said that to me it shifted how I viewed myself. Rather than giving up the fight to resist temptation, my spirit was emboldened to be the person Jesus saw me as. For others, if Jesus sees me as innocent, who is someone else to condemn me? If the King of Kings, the Lord of Lords, the judge of the whole world, sees me as innocent, who are you to condemn me? Do you know my whole story?

Here's another point. If despite my best efforts, I am unable to free myself from bondage, and if freedom only comes by the grace of God, does all the blame land on my shoulders if I am still in sin? Are there institutional, systemic problems that need to be addressed as well? Ravi caught a lot of flak, especially from one of the prophets I follow, saying Ravi was a wolf in sheep's clothing. Was he sexually molested as a child or victim of a sex crime? Do you know his life story? Yes, sin should be exposed so it does not spread in the shadows of secrecy. But who has the right to throw stones? Why did Jesus not stone the woman caught in adultery when she did not confess it first? Do you think God knows more than we do? I'm not excusing sin. Jesus did not ignore her sin. But the answer isn't stoning. If Jesus didn't condemn, who are we to?

Many Christians act like moral, armchair quarterbacks, so quick to throw stones, especially on social media. Remember, Jesus said that if you want to throw stones you better make sure you don't have any sin in your life. Even He did not pick up a stone. Stressing "Go and sin no more" while leaving out the "Neither do I condemn you" part is still throwing stones. Way more work needs to be done to understand this complicated bondage to sexual sin. Flippantly telling people to stop sinning while offering no effort to help is not the answer. Someone has to come alongside to walk them through the healing process of exposure and repentance, and with much grace I might add.

A friend of mine shared Romans 12:2 with me, "Don't copy the behavior and customs of this world, but let God transform you into a new person by changing the way you think. Then you will learn to know God's will for you, which is good and pleasing and perfect." (NLT) He told me that this is essentially like rewiring your mind, the same thing the pastor said in the video I shared earlier. Again, the name of the YouTube video is *A Pastor's Struggle with Pornography and Prostitutes—Gary Wilkerson Podcast—035.*[9] I highly recommend you watch this.

---

[9]Accessed at https://www.youtube.com/watch?v=tjCRR2YT7_I

Anyway, I can see my path ahead of me to freedom. Can you see your path ahead of you? I want to encourage those reading this book that there are answers. I know that it's dark and it's lonely.

Jesus loves you and will forgive you every time you bring your sin to Him. In a way, we addicts are like starving little kids that steal food from shops. Desperation and bondage drive us to steal as well. We're just like those little kids, us addicts, we're just going into the fruit shop stealing food; we can't stop. To begin to fix this, the main issue has to be addressed. The church has to stop hiding sexual sin because they do not want to deal with it.

So, let's start with this: write to me and and tell me your addictions. Simply confess them to me. Better yet, if you know a friend in your church with the same issues, have them read this book and get them in touch with me. My email address is survivors.sanctuary@gmail.com.

My name is Matthew Robert Payne. I have had an addiction to pornography and prostitutes for nearly thirty years. I am a broken man. I do not claim to have the answers. But I do know Jesus. Freedom begins with Him. I believe one day I will be free. And so will you. Let's begin our journey to freedom together.

CLOSING THOUGHTS

In the past week while I was getting the book ready, I came under tremendous demonic attack. Though I have not got answers for you, I do know one thing for certain from the massive spiritual warfare that I went through this week—Satan does not want this book to be published.

We live in a world where Christians hide their sins, and that has to stop. Let me be the first to help by lifting the lid off my life with this very transparent book, sharing my deepest and most regretful sins.

I would encourage you to write to me and confess your sins to me if you have no one else that you can confess to. Feel free to write to me at survivors.sanctuary@gmail.com anytime. I am a survivor of sexual abuse. I will protect your privacy; consider my life to be safe place, a sanctuary. Hence, I have had this "survivors sanctuary" email address for twenty years. Please get in touch.

I'D LOVE TO HEAR FROM YOU

One of the ways that you can bless me as a writer is by writing an honest and candid review of my book on Amazon where you purchased this book. I always read the reviews of my books, and I would love to hear what you have to say about this one.

Before I buy a book, I read the reviews first. You can make an informed decision about a book when you have read enough honest reviews from readers. One way to help me sell this book and to give me positive feedback is by writing a review for me. It doesn't cost you a thing but helps me and the future readers of this book enormously.

To request a life-coaching session, request your own personal prophecy, or receive a personal message from your angel, you can also visit my website at http://personal-prophecy-today.com All of the funds raised through my ministry website go toward the books that I write and self-publish. All of my books are available on Amazon. Just search under "Matthew Robert Payne." All of my Kindle versions are ninety-nine cents. To make my books available to every reader, I made them available for free to read at https://matthewrobertpayne.com.

To write to me about this book or to share any other thoughts, please feel free to contact me at my personal email address: survivors.sanctuary@gmail.com.

You can also friend request me on Facebook at Matthew Robert Payne. Please send me a message if we have no friends in common, as a lot of scammers now send me friend requests.

You can also do me a huge favor and share this book on Facebook as a recommended book to read. This will help me and other readers.

Please do not be afraid to contact me and connect with me. I enjoy speaking my readers and all my best friends have read most of my books over time. I can't contact you as I don't know who you are, but you can contact me.

HOW TO SPONSOR A BOOK PROJECT

If you have been blessed by this book, you might consider sponsoring a book for me. It normally costs at least $1,200 to $1500 to produce each book that I write, depending on the length of the book.

If you seek the Holy Spirit about financing a book for me, I know that the Lord would be eternally grateful to you. Consider how much this book has blessed you, and then think of hundreds or even thousands of people who would be blessed by a book of mine. As you are probably aware, the vast majority of my e-books are ninety-nine cents, which proves to you that book writing is indeed a ministry for me and not a money-making venture. I would be very happy if you supported me in this.

If you have any questions for me or if you want to know what projects I am currently working on that your money might finance, you can write to me at survivors.sanctuary@gmail.com and ask me for more information. I would be pleased to give you additional details about my projects

You can sow any amount to my ministry by simply sending me money via the PayPal link at this address: http://personal-prophecy-today.com/support-my-ministry.

You can be sure that your support, no matter the amount, will be used for the publishing of helpful Christian books for people to read.

ABOUT THE AUTHOR

Matthew Robert Payne, a teacher and prophet, enjoys writing what the Lord puts on his heart to share. He receives great pleasure from interacting with others on Facebook, hearing from people who have read his books, and prophesying over people's lives. He is a passionate lover of and disciple of Jesus Christ. He hopes that as you discover his books, you will intimately come to know Jesus, the Father, and Matthew through his transparent writing style.

Matthew grew up in a traditional Baptist church and gave his heart to Jesus Christ at the tender age of eight years old. But he left home at the age of eighteen, living a wild life for many years and engaging in bad habits and addictions. At twenty-seven, he was baptized in water and, at the same time, baptized in the Holy Spirit. Matthew learned about the five-fold ministry offices and received a revelation of their value in the church for today.

He started his journey as a prophet twenty years ago, learning about this gift and putting it into practice. With thousands of prophecies under his belt, he can confidently prophesy to friends and strangers alike. He has been writing for a number of years and self-published his first book in 2011. Today he spends his time earning money self-publishing and writing many books. He also produces many videos that you can view on YouTube.

You can connect with him on Facebook. You can sow into his book-writing ministry, receive a message from your angel, or even receive your own nine-minute personal prophecy from Matthew at http://personal-prophecy-today.com.

<u>ACKNOWLEDGMENTS</u>

I want to thank Jesus, the Holy Spirit, the Father, and my scribe angel Bethany for the knowledge and wisdom in this book. I live to write books.

I want to thank my friends Mary, Shayne, Dundy, Lisa and others who support me with their love. Your love is priceless to me, a broken man.

I want to thank everyone else who has encouraged me and supported me in friendship, prayer and finances. I want to especially thank those who choose to make a monthly support to my ministry and John who makes a donation every two weeks. This really helps me.

Blurb

The time has come for a prophet like me to lift up the skirt of this secret sin that men struggle with, with a three-fold purpose:

1. To let other addicts know that they are not alone.
2. To shine the light on a church culture that does not allow open confession to allow healing for such sins.
3. To encourage the church to stop throwing stones at their wounded.

WARNING

This book exposes the life of a thirty-year sex addict. Portions of this are not suitable for young audiences. If you are under the age of eighteen, please read no further. It contains graphic sexual content including language, scenarios, and outcomes. The author wrote this book to expose the lifestyle and resulting negative consequences of sex addiction, specifically to prostitutes and pornography. Additionally, even certain adults may find the content offensive. As a result, read at your own risk.